Anonymous

Facts about Armenia

Anonymous

Facts about Armenia

ISBN/EAN: 9783337294724

Printed in Europe, USA, Canada, Australia, Japan

Cover: Foto ©Thomas Meinert / pixelio.de

More available books at **www.hansebooks.com**

ABOUT
ARMENIA.

SASSOON AS REPORTED BY A NATIVE.—MR. GLADSTONE'S SPEECH AND DR. DILLON'S ARTICLE ON ARMENIA.

Publication No. 1, of the Armenian Patriotic Alliance.

NEW YORK:
E. SCOTT CO., PRINTERS AND PUBLISHERS,
146 West 23d Street.
1895.

Notice.

THE United States may well be proud of the noble stand taken by its periodical Press for the Armenian Cause. American journalism has powerfully reacted on the British, and the two have succeeded in stirring such a universal movement of opinion in behalf of outraged Armenia that may be considered perhaps the most comforting sign of this *fin de siecle*.

By his clear declaration in full Parliament as to the "very special kind" of the Sultan's independence, LORD SALISBURY, the Prime Minister, quietly withdrew British support from the Ottoman throne. Abd-ul-Hamid would tremble to the marrow of his bones were he capable of comprehending the full meaning of that solemn declaration. The Press heartily applauded the noble lord, and continues its campaign with encouraged hope. The waves of opinion are now in greater fury roaring around the accursed Porte. According to all indications the thunders shall never hush until the thunderbolt shall strike and consume the disgraceful mechanism which has too long been tolerated to work human misery and demoralization. And that will be indeed a glorious achievement to the credit of the nineteenth century.

This philanthropic movement of opinion was effected by the publication of the facts Since the last Armenian massacre, the horrible character of Turkish misrule has been brought to growing light day after day, and the world stands now convinced that the Government of the Sultan is not merely corrupt and weak, but that all its energies are used to execute the fiendish plan of exterminating the Christian Armenians at their historic home.

The object of the present pamphlet is to throw more light on *the facts*, and to give a wider circulation to the most trustworthy of reports relative to the massacre at Sassoon and the general condition of Armenia.

The report which I have with the greatest care taken from the lips of MR. VARTAN DILLOYAN, is given first. MR. DILLOYAN is a native of the Dalvorig village in Sassoon. He was fortunate enough to escape the bayonet of the Turkish soldiery last summer, and fled to Caucasus. proceeded to England, and after having, as an eye-witness, told in that country the tale of the horrors, has now come to America.

The Sassoon Armenian dialect, as I studied it on the lips of this refugee, is difficult to understand for Armenians. It approaches more than any other provincial dialect the old classic Armenian used for the translation of the Bible in the fifth century. There is a good deal of corruption in the individual words, but the syntax is remarkably well preserved. No such true Armenian is spoken in any other part of Armenia. And as the language, so the Armenian national character has been admirably well preserved in Sassoon, while in Turkey and Persia it has undergone the deplorable impression of fanatic and continuous tyranny. The Armenians of Sassoon are full of physicial and moral courage, dignified, kind, truthful and industrious. They have, withal, a high degree of intellectual capacity. Turkey, unable to corrupt these Armenian highlanders, proceeded to exterminate them, and in doing so, it aimed at the heart of Armenia.

Next to the report of the Sassoonian, the reader will find MR. GLADSTONE'S latest speech on Armenia, somewhat condensed. In that speech of the *Grand Old Man* the heart of the whole Christendom is throbbing with holy indignation.

The third document is the remarkable and remarked article of DR. DILLON, the special Commissioner of the *Daily Telegraph* to Armenia, who spent many months on the grounds in sounding to the bottom the condition of things. He talked with Turkish soldiers, Kurdish chiefs, Armenian prisoners, and put his finger on the wounds of the living victims of Ottoman barbarity. His article on "The Condition of Armenia," in the August number of the *Contemporary Review* is the condensed result of so much painstaking and conscientious labour, and gives a clear, horrifying view of the *whole situation*. We reprint it, nearly entire, by the kind permission of the publishers of the *Review*, to whom our Alliance publicly expresses its sincerest gratitude.

M. S. GABRIEL,
President of the Armenian Patriotic Alliance.

New York, October 1, 1895.

Sassoon.

AS REPORTED BY A NATIVE.

SASSOON is a mountainous province in the southern portion of the Armenian plateau, east of Lake Van. It is inhabited exclusively by Armenians and Kurds, the former race being in majority. There is, however, no intermingling of the races; the Armenian villages are grouped in the centre of the province, and the Kurdish are scattered all around.

The Armenians speak Armenian, the Kurds speak Kurdish. The Armenians are Christians, the Kurds are Mohammedans, and quite fanatic Mohammedans. They often propose to their Armenian friends to adopt "the true religion," with promise of a certain number of Armenian houses to be made tributary to them. But the Armenians are even more ardent believers in Christianity than the Kurds are in Islam, and they would rather lose all, even their lives, than to deny "the *sweet* Christ," as they invariably call him.

Some of the Sassoon Kurds can talk Armenian, but even when talking Armenian, they are easily recognized by the Armenians. The Kurds have the stamp of barbarism on their features and expression.

RELATION BETWEEN THE ARMENIANS AND THE KURDS.

The relation of the Kurd to the Armenian is that of the parasite to the plant.

The Armenians support both themselves and the Kurds, and at the same time pay taxes to the Turkish Government. They suffice to do all this thanks to their wonderful industry. They are farmers, shepherds, artisans and merchants.

Near the village of Dalvorig there are iron mines, which the Armenians work in a primitive fashion, and make ploughs, hatchets, axes, knives, swords, etc. The ploughs made by the Sassoonians are, on account of their superiority, in great demand in Armenia and Kurdistan.

The Sassoonians export their produce, sheep, raisins, honey, silk, iron utensils, to Moosh, Farkin and Diarbekir.

Of all these Armenian goods the Kurds must receive their share, or *besh*, as they call it. The chief or *Agha* of the Kurdish tribe will come every spring, at the head of his men, to collect the tribute of the Armenian villages in sheep, mules, carpets, rugs, stockings, iron implements and the rest.

The Armenians would think themselves fortunate if they had to satisfy only one master, but there are three Kurdish tribes in Sassoon proper—*the Khanuvdulik*, *the Bosuktzik* and *the Ousvi House*—each claiming its own tribute. There are other tribes on the borders of Sassoon in close neighborhood—*the Pakrantzik*, *the Baduktzik*, *the Khisantzik* and *the Belektzik*, besides many other smaller *ashirets*—which demand their share.

The villages of the Dalvorig district, stronger than most others, pay tribute to only seven tribes. Some of the other villages are visited by as many as ten. The village of Havgoonk must sometimes satisfy 12 ashirets. No sooner one chief steps out than another arrives, and thus one after the other make their collections.

TAXES TO THE TURKISH GOVERNMENT.

The principal taxes which the Sassoon Armenians pay to the government, are (1), the Poll-tax, $2.00 per head, including the new-born male baby. (2), Tax on real estate. (3), *Khamtchoori*, namely, 5 piasters per head of sheep—one eighth of the value of the sheep. (4), Tithe of agricultural products.

THE CHANGE.

Despite such continuous spoliation by Kurd and Turk, the Armenians managed to get along tolerably. But in the course of recent years their condition was rendered intolerably worse.

Turk and Kurd became more and more exacting, the Kurd being instructed by the Turk. The Kurds would be satisfied with the traditional tribute, but the Turkish authorities incited them to demand more, to plunder and to kill.

The Kurds, at first unwilling to follow the Turkish policy, told the Armenians, in confidence, what the Osmalis were urging them to do. But the preaching of the Turks did affect gradually the Kurdish mind. They began to impose on the Armenians heavier tributes, hard personal services, and to demand, besides the *besh* in kind, cash also. They attacked sometimes the Armenian caravans and plundered the merchants, they sometimes carried off the Armenian flocks. Friction, quarrel between the two races grew more and more frequent, to the hearty satisfaction of the government.

On the other hand, the Turkish authorities treated more and more unjustly the Sassoonians. The tithe was raised from 10 per cent. to 8 per cent., and from 8 per cent. to 6 5 per cent., and it was to be paid in cash, not in kind as before.

As soon as the Sassoonians entered Moosh or any other city to sell their goods, they would find themselves at the mercy of the Turks. They could not sell to whom they chose. A Turk would approach and agree to pay so much per head of sheep or so much per lb. of honey. The goods would be transported to his house, and then he would pay 25 piasters per head of sheep instead af 40 piasters, and half the sum due for the honey. Of course, the Sassoonian would protest and dispute, but the dispute would end by a good whipping administered by the Turk. The authorities, if resorted to by the Armenian, would make him regret his stupid hope of justice to be got from the government.

In traveling far from their mountains, the Sassoonians would be attacked by Kurdish bands or Turks, near the villages, and would be plundered not only of their goods but also of the mules on which they were loaded.

The Sassoonians would, hands empty and hearts full of bitterness, return home, cursing Kurd and Turk, cursing also the cities as big traps.

Of late years they have abandoned the culture of tobacco, the raising of silk worms and keeping bees, because they could not travel in safety, and when they were not plundered on the plain, they were plundered in the cities, where they had to sell their honey and silk and tobacco and all at the price arbitrarily decided by the Turks.

THE EVENTS OF 1893.

The Sassonians thus impoverished on the one hand and with heavier charges imposed on the other, found themselves in an impossible situation. They had pushed patience and concessions to the last limit beyond which human conscience could not go, as they manfully felt.

The Kurds came early in the Spring of 1893, with demands still more exorbitant than ever before, the chiefs being escorted by an unusally greater number of their men, well armed.

The Armenians of Dalvorig undertook this time to reason more plainly with the Kurds. ' Why do you not," asked they of the Kurds, "treat us as your fathers used to do. You demand from us every year more; besides you behave with us like enemies, you carry off our flocks, you watch our caravans and attack them. Your manifest intention is to ruin us. Now you cannot be our friends and our enimies at the same time. We can endure this no longer."

The Kurds did not understand reason, refused the proposition of the Armenians, and the Armenians refused to pay them any tribute.

The Kurds returned with the intention of coming back in greater force. They held a consultation, and were encouraged by the Turkish authorities.

Three of the tribes, the Pakrantzik, the Khiyantzik and the Baduktzik united their forces, 7 or 8,000 men strong, and marched on Dalvorig.

The Dalvorig Armenians had to protect their villages and flocks against the thieving parties, and to fight at the same time, against the main army. 120 men from Dalvorig went to meet the principal force and stopped its march.

For four days the two armies watched each other. The Armenians were behind the rocks of Furfurkar, scattered. The Kurds also had a strong position. There were 40 Armenian women helping their husbands and brothers by bringing them bread and water and by encouraging them. The Kurds attempted several times to march on and overwhelm the Armenians, but could not endure the Armenian fire. In their last attempt, the son of the Khiyantzi chieftain, Tmig, fell among others, dead. This altogther disheartened the Kurds. They retreated for good.

The Armenians lost five men and one woman. The loss on the Kurdish side was considerable, perhaps a hundred or more. The Kurds carried back their dead or wounded.

The thieving expeditions were more successful. From the villages they carried off thousands of sheep.

As the result of this campaign, the Kurds were once more inspired with fear respecting Dalvorig. Unaided by the Turkish Army, they would not, for some long years, venture to attack again the brave Dalvorig.

On the other hand the unsuccessful attack of the 8,000, was a new revelation to the Porte. The Government saw that there was some respectable Armenian force in Dalvorig.

Troops were sent immediately to Sassoon, which camped a week in the grain fields, and without undertaking any operation, returned to Moosh.

Then came the tax-officer with a number of gendarms and collected the taxes. The Armenians complained to him that the Kurds had carried off their flocks. He promised to have the flocks returned, if the headmen of the villages would go with him to identify the stocks. They did go,—not the headmen, as they could not trust the Turks, but three other villagers—but the Kurds openly told the officer that they had acted according to the plain authorization of the Government to plunder and kill. The Turk got from the Kurds, however, some of the stolen mules and sheep, but kept them for himself. Besides, he did not allow the three Armenians to return, and nobody knew what befell them.

THE MASSACRE OF 1894.

The Armenians of Sassoon were fully aware of the hostile intention of the Government, but they could not imagine it to be one of utter extermination.

The Porte had prepared its plans. Sassoon was doomed.

The Kurds were to come in much greater number, the Government was to furnish them provision and ammunition, and the regular army was to second them in case of need.

The various tribes received invitations to take part in the great expedition, and the chiefs, with their men, arrived one after the other. The total number of the Kurds who took part in the campaign, may be estimated at 30,000. The Armenians believed, in the beginning, that they had to do only with the Kurds. They found out, later, that an Ottoman regular army, with provisions, rifles, cannons and carosene oil, was standing at the back of the Kurds.

The plan was to destroy first Shenig, Semal, Guelliegoozan, Aliantz, etc., and then to proceed toward Dalvorig.

The Kurds, notwithstanding their immense number, proved to be unequal to the task. The Armenians held their own and the Kurds got worsted.

After two weeks fight between Kurd and Armenian, the regular army entered into active campaign.

Mountain pieces began to thunder. The Armenians, having nearly exhausted their ammunition, took to flight.

Kurd and Turk pursued them and massacred men, women and children. The houses were searched and then put on fire.

From certain villages groops of men, tax receipts in their hands, went to the camp and asked to be protected, but were slaughtered.

A great number of villages, outside of the Dalvorig district, which had in no wise been concerned in the conflicts of the previous years, were also attacked to the unspeakable horror of the populations.

The troops climbed up even the Mount Antok, where a multitude of fugitives had taken refuge, and massacred them. A number of women and girls were taken to the church of Gellsegoozan and after being frightfully abused, were tortured to death.

When the work of destruction was nearly accomplished in the other districts, some of the Kurdish armies were sent on Dalvorig. The Dalvorigians defended themselves against the astonishing number of the barbarians, but, after 4 or 5 days, they saw other tribes and regular Turkish troops marching on them on everyhand, and they took to flight.

The scene of the massacre was most horrible. The enemies took a special delight in butchering the Dalvorig people.

An immense crowd of Kurd and Turk soldiery fell upon the Dalvorig village, busy to search the houses, to find out hidden furniture, and then to put fire to the village.

While the troops were so occupied, a number of the fugitives ran as best they could to get out of the Dalvorig district and tried to hide themselves in caves, between rocks or among bushes.

Three days after the complete destruction of the Dalvorig villages, the Kurds and the regular soldiers divided among themselves the result of the plunder, and the Kurds returned to their own mountains.

The regular army yet remained over a week. Soldiers would every day go out to hunt fugitives in the woods and rocks.

My reporter, a native of the Dalvorig village, succeeded in hiding from the searching soldiers, and when, twelve days after the destruction of his home, the army went away, he came out of his hiding place and looked among the corpses for his own dead. He found and buried his father, two nephews and his aunt. He says the bodies were swollen enormously in the sun, and the stench was something awful in all the surroundings. He witnessed many acts of military cruelties which are not proper to be reported.

He thinks, from what he saw himself and heard from other fugitives, that not less than 70 villages, including the smaller ones, were totally or partially destroyed in Sassoon.

Twelve days after Dalvorig was put on fire, he found it yet smoking. The villages of the Dalvorig group were heaps of ruins, and even the fruit trees had been cut down by the army.

After he performed the duty of burying the dead members of his family, he, by night, fled to the Moosh plain, and from there to Caucasus.

M. S. G.

Mr. Gladstone on the Armenian Question.

A MEETING was held in the Town Hall, Chester, England, on the 6th of August, for the purpose of discussing the claims of the Armenians in Turkey. The assembly room at the Town Hall was crowded to excess, and many thousands of persons had to be refused admission.

The duke of Westminster presided, and among those present were a great number of members of Parliament.

MR. GLADSTONE, who was received with prolonged cheers, said:—My Lord Duke, my Lords, and Ladies and Gentlemen,—My first observation shall be a repetition of what has already been said by the noble duke, who has assured you that this meeting is not a meeting called in the interests of any party (hear, hear), or having the smallest connexion with those differences of opinion which naturally and warrantably in this free country will spring up in a complex state of affairs, dividing us on certain questions man from man. (Hear, hear.) But, my lord duke, it is satisfactory to observe that freedom of opinion and even these divisions themselves upon certain questions give increased weight and augmented emphasis to the concurrence of the people to the cordial agreement of the whole nation in these matters where the broad principles of common humanity and common justice prevail. (Cheers.)

A QUESTION OF HUMANITY.

It is perfectly true that the Government whose deeds we have to impeach is a Madomedan Government, and it is perfectly true that the sufferers under those outrages, under those afflictions, are Christian sufferers. The Mahomedan subjects of Turkey suffer a great deal, but what they suffer is only in the way of the ordinary excesses and defects of an intolerably bad Government—perhaps the worst on the face of the earth. (Hear, hear.) That which we have now to do is, I am sorry to say, the opening up of an entirely new chapter. It is not a question of indifferent laws indifferently enforced. It is not a question of administrative violence and administrative abuse. It cuts further and goes to the root of all that concerns human life in its elementary conditions. But this I will say, that if, instead of dealing with the Turkish Government and impeaching it for its misdeeds towards Christian subjects, we were dealing with a Christian Government that was capable of similar misdeeds towards Mahomedan subjects, our indignation ought to be not less, but greater, than it is now. (Cheers.) Well, 1 will take the liberty of reading a resolution which has been placed in my hands and which seems to me to express with firmness, but with moderation, the opinions which I am very confident this meeting will entertain, and this meeting, in entertaining such opinions, is but the representative of the country at large. (Cheers.)

AMERICAN SYMPATHY FOR ARMENIA.

Allow me to go further and to say that the country at large in entertaining these ideas is only a reprentative of civilized humanity, and I will presume to speak on the ground, in part, of personal knowledge, I will presume to speak of the opinions and sympathies that are entertained in that part which is most remote from Armenia—I mean among our own Transatlantic brethren of the United States. If possible, the sentiment in America entertained on the subject of these recent occurences is even more vivid and even stronger, if it can be, than that which beats in the hearts of the people of this country.

THE RESOLUTION.

The terms of the resolution are as follows :

"That this meeting expresses its conviction that her Majesty's Government will have the cordial support of the entire nation, without distinction of party, in any measures which it may adopt for securing to the people of Turkish Armenia such reforms in the administration of that province as shall provide effective guarantees for the safety of life, honour, religion, and property, and that no reforms can be effective which are not placed under the continuous control of the Great Powers of Europe." (Cheers.)

That means, without doubt, the great Powers of Europe, all who choose to combine, and those great Powers which happily have combined and have already, in my judgment, pledged their honour as well as their power to the attainment of the object we have in view. (Cheers.)

THE ATROCITIES PROVED.

Now, it was my fate, I think some six or more months ago, to address a very limited number, not a public assembly, but a limited number of Armenian gentlemen, and gentlemen interested in Armenia on this subject; and at that time I ventured to point out that one of our duties was to avoid premature judgments. There was no authoritative and impartial declaration before the world at that period on the subject of what is known as the Sasun massacre; that massacre to which the noble duke has alluded and with respect to which, horrible as that massacre was, one of the most important witnesses in this case declares that it is thrown into the shade and has become pale and ineffective by the side of the unspeakable horrors which are being enacted from month to month, from week to week, and day to day in the different provinces of Armenia. (Cheers.) It was a duty to avoid premature judgment, and I think it was avoided. There was a great reserve, but at last the engine of dispassionate inquiry was brought to bear, and then it was found that another duty, very important in general in these cases, really in this particular instance had no particular place at all, and though it is a duty to avoid exaggeration, a most sacred duty, it is a duty that has little or no place in the case before us, because it is too well known that the powers of language hardly suffice to describe what has been and is being done, and that exaggeration, if we were ever so much disposed to it, is in such a case really beyond our power. (Cheers.) Those are dreadful words to speak. It is a painful office to perform, and nothing but a strong sense of duty could gather us together between these walls or could induce a man of my age and a man who is not wholly without other difficulties to contend with to resign for the moment that repose and quietude which is the last of many great earthly blessings remaining to him in order to invite you to enter into a consideration of this question—I will not say in order to invite you to allow yourselves to be flooded with the sickening details that it involves. I shall not attempt to lead you into that dreadful field, but I make this appeal to you. I do hope that every one of you will for himself and herself endeavour in such a degree as your position may allow of you to endeavour to acquire some acquaintance with them (hear, hear), because I know that, when I say that a case of this kind puts exaggeration out of the question, I am making a very broad assertion, which would in most cases be violent, which would in all ordinary cases be unwarrantable. But those who will go through the process I have described, or even a limited portion of the process, will find that the words are not too strong for the occasion. (Cheers.) What witnesses ought we to call before us? I should be disposed to say that it matters very little what witness you call. So far as the character of the testimony you will receive is concerned the witnesses are all agreed. At the time that I have just spoken of, six or eight months ago, they were private witnesses. Since that time, although we have not seen the detailed documents of public authority, yet we know that all the broader statements which had been made up to that time and which have made the blood of this nation run cold have been confirmed and verified. They have not been overstated, not withdrawn, not qualified, not reduced, but confirmed in all their breadth, in all their horrible substance, in all their sickening details. (Hear, hear.)

AMERICAN WITNESSES.

And here I may say that it is not merely European witnesses with whom we have to deal. We have American witnesses also in the field, and the testimony of the American witnesses is the same as that of the European; but it is of still greater importance, and for this reason—that everybody knows that America has no separate or sinister political interest of any kind in the affairs of the Levant. She comes into court perfectly honest and perfectly unsuspected and that which she says possesses on that account a double weight. I will not refer to the witnesses in particular, as I have been told you will receive a statement by my reverend friend Canon McColl, who is one of them (cheers); but I believe they are absolutely agreed, that there is no shade of difference prevailing among them.

DR. DILLON.

I will refer to the last of these witnesses, one whom I must say I am disposed to name with honour, it is Dr. Dillon (cheers), whose name has appeared within the last three or four days at the foot of an article of unusual length—Ah! and good were the reasons for extending it to an unusual length—in the *Contemporary Review*. (Cheers.) Perhaps you will ask, as I asked, "Who is Dr. Dillon?" and I am able to describe him to his honour. Dr. Dillon is a man who, as the special commissioner of the *Daily Telegraph* newspaper, some months ago with care and labour, and with the hazard of his life (hear, hear), went into Turkey, laudably making use of a disguise for the purpose, and went into Armenia, so that he might make himself thoroughly master of the facts. (Cheers.) He published his results before any public authority had given utterance to its judgments and those results which he, I rather think, was the first to give to the world in a connected shape—at any rate he was very early in the field—those results have been completely confirmed and established by the inquiries of the delegates appointed by the three Powers— England, France and Russia. (Cheers.) I say he has, at the risk of his life, acquired a title to be believed, and here he gives us an account which bears upon it all the marks of truth, but which, at the same time that we must believe it to be true, you would say is hardly credible. Unhappily some of those matters which are not credible do, in this strange and wayward world of ours, turn out to be true; and here it is hardly credible that there can dwell in the human form a spirit of such intense and diabolical wickedness as is unhappily displayed in some of the narratives Dr. Dillon has laid before the world. I shall not quote from them in detail though I mean to make a single citation, which will be a citation, if I may say so, rather of principle than of detail. I shall not quote the details, but I will say to you that when you begin to read them you will see the truth of what I just now said—namely that we are not dealing at all with a common and ordinary question of abuses of government or the defects of them. We are dealing with something that goes far deeper, far wider, and that imposes upon us and upon you far heavier obligations.

THE FOUR CRIMES.

The whole substance of this remarkable article—and it agrees, as I have said, with the testimony of the other witnesses—I am quoting it because it is the latest—the whole substance of this article may be summed up in four awful words—plunder, murder, rape and torture. ("Shame.") Every incident turns upon one or upon several of those awful words. Plunder and murder you would think are bad enough, but plunder and murder are almost venial by the side of the work of the ravisher and the work of the torturer, as it is described in these pages, and as it is now fully and authentically known to be going on. I will keep my word, and I will not be tempted by—what shall I say?—the dramatic interest attached to such exaggeration of human action as we find here to travel into the details of the facts. they are fitter for private perusal than they are for public discussion. I will not be tempted to travel into them; I will ask you for a moment, any of you who have not yourselves verified the particulars of the case, to credit me with speaking the truth, until I go on to consider who are the doers of these deeds. In all ordinary cases when we have before us instances of crime, perhaps of very horrible crime—for example, there is a sad story in the papers to-day of a massacre in a portion of China—we at once assume that in all countries, unfortunately, there are malefactors, there are plunderers whose deeds we are going to consider. Here, my lord duke, it is nothing of the kind; we have nothing to do here with what are called the dangerous classes of the community; it is not their proceedings which you are asked to consider; it is the proceedings of the Government of Constantinople and its agents. (Cheers.)

THE TURKISH GOVERNMENT RESPONSIBLE.

There is not one of these misdeeds for which the Government at Constantinople is not morally responsible. (Cheers.) Now, who are these agents? Let me tell you very briefly. They fall into three classes. The first have been mentioned by the noble duke—namely the savage Kurds, who are, unhappily, the neighbors of the Armenians, the Armenians being the representatives of one of the oldest civilized Christian races, and being beyond all doubt one of the most pacific, one of the most industrious, and one of the most intelligent races in the world. (Cheers.) These Kurds are by them; they are wild, savage clans. There was but one word, my lord duke, in your address that I should have been disposed to literally criticize, and it was the expression that fell from you that the Sultan had "organized" hese Kurds. They are, in my belief, in no sense organized—that is to say there is no more organization among them than is to be found, say, in a band of robbers; they have no other organization, being nothing but a band of robbers. (Cheers.) These the Sultan and the Government at Constantinople have enrolled, though in a nominal fashion, not with at military discipline, into pretended cavalry regiment and then set them loose with the authority of soldiers of the Sultan to harry and destroy the people of Armenia. (Cheers.) Well, these

Kurds are the first of the agents in this horrible business; the next are the Turkish soldiers, who are in no sense behind the Kurds in their performances; the third are the peace officers, the police and the tax gatherers of the Turkish Government; and there seems to be a deadly competition among all these classes which shall most prove itself an adept in the horrible and infernal work that is before them, but above them and more guilty than they, are the higher officers of the Turkish Government. You will find, if you look into this paper of Dr. Dillon's, that at every point he has exposed himself to confutation if what he says is inaccurate or untrue. He gives names, titles, places, dates, every particular which would enable the Turkish Government to track him out and detect him and hold him up to public reprobation. You will never hear of an answer from the Turkish Government to that article. That may be a bold thing for me to say; but I am confident you will never hear an answer from them which shall follow these statements of Dr. Dillon's, based on his own personal experience, through the details, and attempt to shake the fabric of greviously composed materials which he has built up in the face of the world.

THREE PROPOSITIONS.

I THINK there are certain matters, such as those which have been discussed to-day and discussed in many other forms, on which it is perfectly possible to make up our minds. And what I should say is, that the whole position may be summed up in three brief propositions. I do not know to which of these propositions to assign the less or the greater importance. It appears to me that they are probably each and every one of them absolutely indispensable. The first proposition is this, You ought to moderate your demands. You ought to ask for nothing but that which is strictly necessary, and that possibly according to all that we know of the proposals before us, the rule has been rigidly complied with. I do not hesitate to say, ladies and gentlemen, that the cleanest and clearest method of dealing with this subject, if we should have done it, would have been to tell the Turk to march out of Armenia. (Loud cheers). He has no right to remain there, and it would have been an excellent settlement of the question. But it is by no means certain that Europe or even the three Powers would have been unanimous in seeking after that end. Therefore, let us part with everything except what is known to be indispensable. Then I come to the other two rules, and of these the first is that you should accept no Turkish promises (Hear, hear). They are absolutely and entirely worthless. They are worse than worthless, because they may serve to elude a few persons who, without information or experience, naturally would suppose, when promises are given, that there is something like an intention of fulfilment. Recollect that no scheme is worth having unless it be supported by efficient guarantees entirely outside the promises of the Turkish Government. (Applause). There is another word which I must speak, and it is this: Don't be to much afraid if you hear introduced into this discussion a word that I admit, in ordinary cases, ought to be excluded from all diplomatic proceeding, namely, the word coercion. Coercion is a word perfectly well understood in Constantinople, and it is a word highly appreciated in Constanstinople. It is a drastic dose—(laughter)—which never fails of its aim when it is administered in that quarter. (Laughter) Gentlemen, I would not use these words if I had not myself personally had large and close experience of the proceedings of the Turkish Government. I say, first make your case good, and when your case is made good, determine that it shall prevail. (Cheers). Grammar has something to do with this case. Recollect that while the word "ought" sounded in Constantinople, passes in thin air, and has no force or solidity whatever attaching to it; on the contrary, the brother or sister monosyllable, the word "must" is perfectly understood— (cheers)—and it is a known fact supported by positive experience, which can be verified upon the map of Europe, that a timely and judicious use of ths word never fails for its effect. (Cheers). Gentlemen, I must point out to you that we have reached a very critical position indeed. How are three great Governments in Europe, ruling a population of more than two hundred million souls, with perhaps eight or ten times the population of Turkey, with twenty times the wealth of Turkey, with fifty times the the influence and power of Turkey, who have committed themselves in this matter before the world, I put it to you that if they recede before an irrational resistance —and remember that I have in the first instance postulated that our demands should be reasonable—if they recede before the irrational resistance of the Sultan and the Ottoman Government they are disgraced in the face of the world. Every motive of duty coincides with every motive of self respect, and, my lord duke, you yourself let drop a word which is a frightful word, unhappily not wholly out of place, the word

"EXTERMINATION."

There has gone abroad, I don't say that I feel myself competent to judge the matter, I don't think I do, but there has gone abroad and there is widely entertained a belief that the recent proceedings of the Turkish Government in Armenia particularly, but not in Armenia exclusively, are founded upon deliberate determination to exterminate the Christians in that Empire. I hope it is not true, but at the same time I must say that there are evidences tending to support it—(hear, hear)—and the grand evidence which tends to support it is this: the perfect infatuation of the Turkish Goverment. Now, in my time there have been periods when Turkey was ruled by men of honesty and ability. I will say that until about thirty years ago you could trust the word of the Turkish Government as well as any Government in Europe, you might not approve of their proceedings, but you could trust their word; but a kind of judicial infatuation appears to have come down upon them. What has happened in Turkey? To hear of this vaunting on the part of its Government, and this game of brag that is from time to time being played, that it cannot compromise its dignity, it cannot waive any of its rights. What would come of its rights in one third part of its empire? Within my lifetime Turkey has been reduced by one-third part of her territory, and sixteen or eighteen millions of people inhabiting some of the most beautiful and formerly most famous countries in the world who were under the Ottoman rule are now as free as we are. (Cheers). The Ottoman Government are as well aware of that as we, and yet we find it pursuing these insane courses. On the other hand, my lord Duke most judiciously referred to the plan of Government that was introduced in the Lebanon about 1861, whereby a reasonable share of stability to local institutions and popular control has been given in Turkey, and the results have been most satisfactory. There is also a part of the country, although not a very large part, where something like local self-government is permitted, and it has been very hopeful in its character. But when we see these things—on the one hand that these experiments in a sense of justice have all succeeded and that when adapted to the Greeks and the Bulgarians and four of five other States have resulted in the loss of those States, then I say that the Turkish Government is evidently in such a state of infatuation that it is fain to believe it may, under certain circumstances, be infatuated enough to scheme the extermination of the Christian population. Well, this is a sad and terrible story, and I have been a very long time in telling it, but a very small part of it, but I hope that, having heard the terms of the resolution that will be submitted to you, you will agree that a case is made out. (Cheers). I for one, for the sake of avoiding other complications, would rejoice if the Government of Turkey would come to its senses. If only men like Friad Pacha and Ali Pacha who were in the Government of Turkey after the Crimean War, could be raised from the dead and could inspire the Turkish policy with their spirit and with their principles! That is, in my opinion, what we ought all to desire, and thought it would be more agreeable to clear Turkey than to find her guilty of these terrible charges, yet if we have the smallest regard to humanity, if we are sensible at all of what is due to our own honour after the steps which have been taken within the last twelve or eighteen moths, we must interfere. We must be careful to demand no more than what is just—but at least as much as is necessary—and we must be determined that, with the help of God that which is necessary, and that which is just shall be done, whether there will be a response or whether there be none. (Loud cheers).

The Condition of Armenia.

By E J. DILLON.

A PRETTY story is told of a little girl, who, fearing to lie in bed in the dark, begged her mother not to take the candle away until sleep should render it needless. "What are you afraid of, darling?" asked the strong-minded parent. "Of darkness," was the reply. "But remember, dear, that God is here in the room with you, and God is light itself. He will stay with you all night to keep you company." The silence that followed this dogmatic announcement seemed to show that the intended effect had been produced, until it was softly broken by the sweet voice of the child: " Then, please mamma, take God away and leave the candle."

The attitude of the Armenian population in Turkey towards the humane peoples of Western Europe who, to fiendish tortures and bloody massacres, hopefully oppose well-timed expressions of righteous indignation and moral sympathy, offers considerable analogy to the frame of mind of that untutored child. "We can dispense with your sympathy and pity if only you guarantee us security for life and property." So reasons the grateful Armenian. The impartial outsider, acquainted with the horrible condition of country and people, would naturally go a step further, and fearlessly affirm that the expression of sympathy at public meetings, followed, as in England, by supine inactivity, is not merely inferior to effective material aid, but is positively disastrous. Formerly the Turks disliked the Armenians, and the blood-bath of Sassoun offers a fair indication of the vehemence of their feeling. At present, after the wanton humiliation inflicted upon them by the European friends of their victims, they loathe the very name of Armenia, and deem no cruelties sufficient to satisfy their outraged self-love. The Vali (Governor-General) of Erzeroum, when the foreign consuls of that city lately brought an unusually crying case of injustice to his notice, told the Dragomans that the Turkish Government and Armenian people stood to each other in the relation of husband and wife, and that outsiders who felt pity for the wife when her husband maltreated her, would do wisely and well to abstain from interfering. And the remark is quite true, *if the pair are to go on living together ;* for the brutal husband can always choose his own time and place to vent his feelings on his helpless mate. And this is what is being actually done in Turkish Armenia. Under the eyes of the Russian, English, and French delegates at Moush, the witnesses who had the courage to speak the truth to the representatives of the Powers were thrown into prison, and not a hand was raised to protect them; and at the present moment, within a stone's throw of the foreign consuls and missionaries, loyal Armenians are being hung up by the heels, the hair of their heads and beards plucked out one by one, their bodies branded with red-hot irons and defiled in beastly ways that can neither be described nor hinted at in England, their wives dishonoured in their presence, and their daughters raped before their eyes. And all that the philanthropic English nation has to offer these its *protégés*, is eloquent indignation and barren sympathy. Would it not have been much more benevolent to hush up the massacre of Sassoun and ignore the Pits of Death than to irritate the Turk to the point of madness and then leave him free to vent his fury upon Christians who are shielded only by our sentimental eloquence?

And yet the duty of this country is simplicity itself; we should either put a speedy end to the horrors of Turkish Dahomey or publicly proclaim our inability to fulfil our obligations in Armenia, at the same time repudiating our gigantic engagement to maintain the integrity of the Turkish Empire in Asia. For as it was a grievous blunder to raise this Armenian Question last winter without having first made sure that we could work it out to a satisfactory issue, it is little less than a crime to give the Turks the needful time to carry out their nefarious plans by our obstinate refusal to look the facts in the face.

Those who are familiar with the condition of the five provinces and their Christian inhabitants will unhesitatingly acquiesce in this view of the subject; for those who are not, the following brief sketch may prove instructive.

Turkey's real sway in Armenia dates from the year 1847, when Osman Pasha gave the final *coup de grâce* to the secular power of the Koordish Derebeks in the five south-eastern provinces (Van, Bitlis, Moush, Bayazed, and Diarbekir). During that long spell of nearly fifty years, we can clearly distinguish two periods: one of shameful misgovernment (1847–1891), and the other (1892–1894) of frank extermination. Suasion or remonstrance may do much to remedy the abuses that flow from the former system; force alone can achieve anything against the latter. And in this sense Lord Salisbury's recently expressed view of the matter is absolutely correct.

In the year 1891 the Sublime Porte fearing serious dangers from the promised introduction of reforms into Armenia, and from the anticipated hostility in war time of the Christians living in provinces bordering upon Russia, resolved to kill two birds with one stone, and created the so-called Hamidieh cavalry, composed exclusively of Koords. It was an application of the principle, on which rebels and and rioters throw open the prison doors and invite convicts to rob and kill the members of the upper classes. The plan as propounded by some of the highest officials of the Empire was that the Armenians were to be driven out of the border lands, such as Alashkerd, their places to be taken by Mohammedans, that their numbers in all the five provinces were to be so considerably reduced that the need of special reforms for them should pass away, and that in case of war the Koords should act as a counterweight to the Cossacks.

This plain policy of extermination has been faithfully carried out and considerably extended from that day to this, and unless speedily arrested, will undoubtedly lead to a final solution of the Armenian problem. But a solution which will disgrace Christianity and laugh civilization to scorn. The enlisted Koords were left in their native places, exempted from service, supplied with arms, invested with the inviolability of ambassadors, and paid with the regularity characteristic of the Sublime Porte. And they fulfilled their mission with scrupulous exactness : robbing rich Armenians, looting houses, burning corn and hay, raiding villages, lifting cattle, raping young girls of tender age, dishonouring married women, driving away entire populations, and killing all who were manly or mad enough to attempt to resist. Armenians are now among the poorest and most wretched people on the globe.

Perhaps the Turkish authorities did not foresee, nor Turkish justice approve, these results? The authorities not only expected them, but aided and abetted, incited and rewarded those who actually committed them; and whenever an Armenian dared to complain, not only was he not listened to by the officials whom he paid to protect him, but he was thrown into a fetid prison and tortured and outraged in strange and horrible ways for his presumption and insolence.

The massacre of Sassoun itself is now proved to have been the deliberate deed of the representatives of the Sublime Porte, carefully planned and unflinchingly executed in spite of the squeamishness of Koordish brigands and the fitful gleams of human nature that occasionally made themselves felt in the hearts even of Turkish soldiers.

To complain, therefore, of the insecurity of life and property in Armenia, so long as the country is irresponsibly governed by the Sublime Porte, is as reasonable as it would be for a soldier to object to the great danger to life and limb from the enemy's bullets during a sanguinary engagement. The result complained of is precisely the object aimed at, and its completeness the most conclusive proof of the efficiency of the means employed. An eminent foreign statesman who is commonly credited with Turcophile sentiments of uncompromising thoroughness, lately remarked to me in private conversation that Turkish rule in Armenia might be aptly described as organized brigandage, legalized murder, and meritorious immorality. Protests against such a system may be right and proper, but they can hardly be considered profitable. A philanthropist visiting a prison may feel shocked when he discovers one of the convicts with his hands and feet tied with cords; but he will scarcely spend time in complaining if he learns that the prisoner has been condemned to death, and is about to be hanged by the executioner.

The first step in carrying out the Plan of Extermination was the systematic impoverishment of the people. This is natural in a country whose officials are kept waiting eight or ten months for their salaries, and must then content themselves with but a fraction of what is due. "I have not received a para* for the past twenty weeks, and I cannot buy even clothes," exclaimed the official who was told off to "shadow" me day and night in Erzeroum. "Do they pay you your salary regularly?" I inquired of the head of the telegraph office at Kutek. "No, Effendi, not regularly," he replied; "I have not had anything now for fully eight months. Oh yes, I have; a month's salary was given to me at Bairam."† "How do you manage to live, then?" "Poorly." "But you must have some money to go on with, or else you could not keep body and soul together?" "I have a little, of course, but not enough. Allah is good. You have now given me some money yourself." "Yes, but that is not for you; it is for telegrams, and belongs to the State." "Well, my shadow will have grown considerably less before the State beholds the gleam of it. I keep for myself all money paid in by the public. I take it as instalments of my salary. It does not amount to very much. But whatever it happens to be, I pocket it." These men are, of course, petty officials, but their case is not essentially different from that of the majority of their betters, and judges, officers, deputy-governors, and valis, etc., etc., are to the full as impecunious and incomparably more greedy.

Tahsin Pasha, the late Governor-General of Bitlis, is a fair specimen of the high Turkish dignitary of the epoch of extermination. An avaricious skinflint, he was as cruel as Ugolino's enemy, Ruggieri, and as cold as Captain Maleger in Spenser's "Faëry Queen." He cultivated a habit of imprisoning scores of wealthy Armenians, without any imputed charge or show of pretext. Liberty was then offered them in return for exorbitant sums representing the greater part of their substance. Refusal to pay was followed by treatment compared with which the torture of the Jews in mediæval England, or the agonies of the eunuchs of the princesses of Oude in modern India were mild and salutary chastisements. Some men were kept standing up all day and night, forbidden to eat, drink, or move. If they lost strength and consciousness, cold water or hot irons soon brought them round, and the work of coercion continued. Time and perseverance being on the side of the Turks, the Armenians generally ended by sacrificing everything that made life valuable, for the sake of exemption from maddening pain. It was a case of sacrificing or being

---

*A Turkish coin. Forty paras are equivalent to twopence.
†Bairam is the festival which follows the long fast of Ramazan.

sacrificed, and that which seemed the lesser of the two evils was invariably chosen.

In the Vilayet of Bitlis several hundred Armenians who possessed money, cattle or crops, were arbitrarily imprisoned and set free on the payment of large bribes. Some of them, unable to produce the money at once, were kept in the noisome dungeons until they raised the sum demanded, or were released by death. About one hundred Armenian prisoners died in the prison of Bitlis alone. The following petition signed and sent to me—and if I mistake not, also to the foreign delegates at Moush—from a well-known man whose name and address I publish, will help to convey some idea of how the Vali of Bitlis governed his province, and prospered the while: "We, who have served the Turkish Government with absolute loyalty, are maltreated and oppressed, more particularly of late years, now by the Government itself, now by Koordish brigands. Thus last year (1894) I was suddenly arrested at my own house by Turkish police and gendarmes, who escorted me to the prison of Bitlis, where I was insulted and subjected to the most horrible tortures. Having been kept four months there, I was released on condition of paying £450, by way of ransom. No reason, no pretext has been given for this treatment. On my return home, I found my house in disorder, my affairs ruined, my means gone. My first thought was to appeal to the Turkish Government for redress, but I shrank from doing so, lest I should be condemned again. Hearing that you have come to Armenia for the purpose of investigating the condition of the people, I venture to request you, in God's name, to take notice of the facts of my case. Signed, Boghos Darmanian, of the village of Iknakhodja of the Kaza of Manazkerd."

In 1890, the village elder of Odandjor in Boolanyk, Abdal by name, was a wealthy man, as wealth goes in that part of the world. He possessed 50 buffaloes, 80 oxen, 600 sheep, besides horses, etc. The women of his family wore golden ornaments in their hair and on their breast, and he paid £50 a year in taxes to the treasury. That was in 1890. In 1894 he was a poverty-stricken peasant, familiar with misery and apprehensive of death from hunger. His village and those of the entire district had been plundered, and the inhabitants stripped, so to say, naked, the Turkish authorities smiling approval the while. During the year 1894, in the districts of Boolanyk and Moush alone, upwards of ten thousand head of cattle and sheep were driven off by the Koords.

This was the method in vogue all over the country; the details varied according to the condition of things, places, and kinglets, but the means and end never varied. The result is the utter disappearance of wealth and the rapid spread of misery, so intense, so irremediable, so utterly loathsome in its moral and physical effects as to have inspired some of its victims with that wild courage akin to madness which always takes its rise in despair.*

Retween the Vali or Governor-General and the Zaptieh or tax-gatherer the rungs of the administrative ladder are many, and to each and all of them some portion of the substance of industrious Armenians adheres. No doubt there are far worse things than the loss of one's property, and unemotional Englishmen would rather save their sympathy for those who have endured them. But surely even that is bad enough when the outcome not of crime, accident, or carelessness, but of shameless and defiant injustice, and where the loser has a family of some fifteen to twenty persons. And that the loss of property very often entailed far greater losses will be evident from some of the following facts.

In July, 1892, a captain of his Majesty's Hamidieh Cavalry, Idris by name, an ornament of the Hassnanlee tribe, came with his brother to demand a contribution of fodder from the inhabitants of Hamsisheikh. They accosted two of the Armenian notables, Alo and Hatchadoor, and ordered them to provide the hay required. "We do not possess such a quantity in the whole village," they replied. "Produce the hay without more ado, or I'll shoot you dead," exclaimed Idris. "But it does not exist, and we cannot create it." "Then die," said the gallant captain, and shot them dead on the spot. A formal complaint was lodged against Idris, and the Kaimakam, to his credit, arrested him and kept him in prison for four weeks, when the valiant Koord having paid the usual bribe was set at liberty. About thirty similar murders were committed in the same district of Boolanyk during that season, with the same publicity and the same impunity.

At first the Armenians were wont to complain when their relatives or friends were killed, in the hope that in some cases the arm of the law might be raised to punish the murderers and thus produce a deterrent effect upon others who might feel disposed to go and do likewise. But they were very soon weaned of this habit, by methods the nature of which may be gathered from the following incident: In July, 1892, a Koord named Ahmed Ogloo Batal rode over to Govandook (District of Khnouss) and drove off four oxen belonging to an Armenian named Mookho. In 1892 the law forbidding Christians to carry arms was not yet strictly observed, and Mookho possessing a revolver, and seeing that the Koord was about to use his, fired. Both weapons went off at once and both men fell dead on the spot. What then happened was this : Nineteen Armenians of the village, none of whom had any knowledge of what had occurred, were arrested and

---

*I have published elsewhere a comparison between the prosperity of Armenians who lived in the epoch of misgovernment and the indigence of those who languish in the present era of extermination, but this interesting subject has never been exhaustively treated.

put in jail and told that they would be released on payment of a heavy bribe. Ten paid it and were set free at once. The remainder, refusing, were kept in prison for a long time afterwards. None of the Koords were molested. "Why should Mohammedans be punished for killing Armenians?" asked a Koordish brigand who was also a Hamidieh officer, of me. "It is unheard of." Why indeed? That the relatives of the murdered people should be punished and punished severely for complaining of those who have made them widows or orphans seems meet and proper to the Mohammedan mind—perhaps because it is usual.

In August, 1893, the Djibranlee Koords attacked the village of Kaghkik, plundered it, and wounded a merchant named Oannes, who was engaged in business in his shop. Next day Oannes went to the Deputy Governor (Kaimakam) in Khnoussaberd and lodged a complaint, whereupon the Kaimakam put him in prison for "lying." The sufferings inflicted upon him in that hotbed of typhoid fever exceed belief—but that is another story. After eight days his neighbours brought a Koord before the Kaimakam who bore out their evidence that Oannes had been really wounded in the manner described. and that he was not lying. Then, and then only, the authorities *allowed the people* to pay a bribe of ten pounds for the release of the wounded man.

The inhabitants of Krtaboz (a village in Bassen) told me several horrible stories of what they had to endure lately from the Koords, who drove off their twenty-three oxen, twenty-eight horses, sixty cows, and twenty sheep. One which illustrates the method of *Turkish* justice will suffice to give the reader an inkling of their nature. "Last May (1894) twelve mounted Hamidiehs attacked our village and seized our priest, Der David. They promised to release him if he paid them six pounds. He borrowed the sum, gave it to his captors, and was set free. The troops fired upon the other villagers, who ran away. Next day Guil Beg went to Hassankaleh to complain to the authorities. They abused him, called him a liar, and ordered him to be imprisoned. After having spent forty days in the horrible hole called a prison, he was permitted to pay a bribe of seven pounds and go home."

There is no redress whatever for a Christian who has suffered in property, limb, or life at the hands of Mohammedans; not because the law officers are careless or lethargic, but, because they are specially retained on the other side. And the proof of this, if any proof were needed, is that the complainants themselves are speedily punished for lodging an information against their persecutors. But whenever a Koord or a Turk is the victim of a "crime," or even an accident, the energy of the Government officials knows no bounds. In the spring of last year, when the snows were thawing and the waters rose high in the rivers and streams, some needy Koords were moving along the bank of the river, hard by Hussnaker. They were wretched beggars, asking alms, and battling with fate. In an attempt to ford the river they were carried away and drowned. Forthwith the villagers were accused of having murdered them, and four Armenian notables were arrested and imprisoned in Hassankaleh on this trumpery charge, the real object of which was not disguised. After the lapse of seven or eight months the villagers were told that on payment of a bribe of £75 the prisoners would be discharged. The money had to be scraped together and paid to the authorities, whereupon the men were released. I saw two of them, Atam and Dono, myself.

The taxes levied upon Armenians are exorbitant; the bribes that invariably accompany them, and are imposed by the Zaptiehs, may swell to any proportions, and resume the most repugnant forms, while the methods employed to collect both constitute by themselves a sufficient justification for the sweeping away of Ottoman rule in Armenia.

To give a fair instance of the different rates of taxation for Christians and Mohammedans in towns it will suffice to point out that in Erzeroum, where there are 8,000 Mohammedan houses, the Moslems pay only 395,000 piastres, whereas the Christians, whose houses number but 2,000, pay 430,000 piastres.

In the country districts everything, without exception, is highly taxed by the Government, and the heaviest burden of this legal exaction is light when compared with the extortion practiced by its agents, the Zaptiehs. A family, for instance, is supposed to contribute, say, £5, and fulfils its obligation. The Zaptiehs, however, ask for £3 or £4 more for themselves, and are met with a rash refusal Negotiations, interlarded with violent and abusive language, ensue, and £1 is accepted. But the Zaptiehs' blood is up. In a week they return and demand the same taxes over again. The Armenians wax angry, protest and present their receipt; whereat the Zaptiehs laughingly explain that the document in question is no receipt but a few verses from a Turkish book. The villagers plead poverty and implore mercy. Greed, not compassion, moves the Zaptiehs to compromise the matter for £3 more, but the money is not forthcoming. Then they demand the surrender of the young women and girls of the family to glut their brutal appetites, and refusal is punished with a series of tortures over which decency and humanity throw a veil of silence Rape, and every kind of brutal outrage conceivable to the diseased mind of Oriental profligates, and incredible to the average European intelligence, varied perhaps with murder or arson, wind up the incident.

I have seen and spoken with victims of these representatives of the Sublime Porte ; I have inspected their wounds, questioned their families, interrogated their priests, their persecutors, and their gaolers (some of them being incarcerated for complaining), and I unhesitatingly affirm, not merely that these horrors are real facts, but that they are frequent occurrences. The following is the translation of an authentic document in my possession, signed and sealed by the inhabitants of Melikan (Kaza of Keghi), addressed as recently as March 26th of the present year to his Beatitude, the learned and saintly Metropolitan Archbishop of Erzeroum, a dignitary who enjoys the respect and esteem of friends and foes:

" For a long time past the four or five Zaptiehs charged with the collection of the imperial taxes have chosen our village for their headquarters, and compel the inhabitants of the outlying country to come hither to pay their contributions They eat, drink, and feed their horses at our expense, undisguisedly showing that they are resolved to reduce us to beggary.

"Lately seven other Zaptiehs, who had not even the pretext of collecting the taxes, entered our village, beat the inhabitants, insulted the Christian religion, and dishonoured our wives and daughters, after which they seized three men who protested—Boghos, Mardig, and Krikor—bound them with a twofold chain, and hung them up by the feet from the rafters. They left them in this position until the blood began to flow from their nostrils. These poor men fell ill in consequence. The Zaptiehs, however, declared publicly that they had treated the people thus merely in obedience to the special orders of the chief of the police.

" We therefore appeal to imperial justice to rescue us from this unbearable position. The inhabitants of the village of Melikan, Kaza of Keghi.   (Signed)   KATSHERE.
" 26th March, 1895."

Here is another petition from another village of the same Kaza, likewise addressed to the Metropolitan Archbishop of Erzeroum:

"A number of Zaptiehs, on pretext of gathering the taxes, rode into our village at five o'clock Turkish (about 10 o'clock A. M.) broke open the doors of our dwellings, entered the inner apartments, clutched our wives and children, who were in a state of semi-nudity, and cast them into the road along with the couches on which they lay. Then they beat and maltreated them most cruelly. Finally they selected over thirty of our women, shut them up in a barn, and wrought their criminal will upon them. Before leaving they took all the food and fodder we possessed, as is their invariable custom. We beg to draw your attention to these facts, and to implore the imperial clemency. The inhabitants of the village of Arek, Kaza of Keghi.
      (Signed)   MOORADIAN, RESSIAN, BERGHOYAN, MELKONIAN.
" 26th March, 1895."

I was present myself in the house of an Armenian peasant, of the village of Kipri Kieu, when a number of mounted Zaptiehs arrived, woke up the inmates, and insolently demanded food for themselves, barley for their horses, and couches for the night. What more they would have called for I am not prepared to say, but I extricated my host from the difficulty by refusing them admittance on the ground that I had hired the house for the night. No wonder that the peasants of the District of Khnouss complain, in the petition which they asked me to lay before "the noble and humane people of England," "That the once prosperous and fertile country is now deserted, waste and desolate."

These, then, are the horrors which are connoted by the phrase so flippantly uttered by certain enlightened English people: "These Armenians and Koords are eternally quarrelling, and a little bloodshed more or less would not seem seriously to affect the general average." It is true enough in the sense in which it is correct to say that sheep and wolves are perpetually at war with each other, and in this sense only. The Armenians are naturally peaceful in all places: passionately devoted to agriculture in the country, and wholly absorbed by mercantile pursuits in the towns. Lest their inborn aversion to bloodshed, however, should be overcome by the impulse of duty, the instinct of self-defense, or deep-rooted affection for those near and dear to them, they are forbidden to possess arms, and the tortures that are inflicted on the few who disregard this law, would bring a blush to the cheek of a countryman of Confucius.* They must rely for protection exclusively upon the Turkish soldiers and the Turkish law.

The nature of the protection afforded by the Imperial troops was sufficiently clearly revealed last August and September on the slopes of Frfrkar and the heights of Andok, in the hamlets of Dalvorik and in the valley of Ghellyegoozan. The villages of Odandjor, Hamzasheikh, Kakarloob Kharagyul, flourishing and prosperous in 1890–1891, did not contain one sheep, one buffalo, one horse in 1894. The stables were all tenantless, the stalls all empty, and the ashes of seventy enormous stacks of corn told the rest of the tale. This was the congenial work of the Koords, whose friends, the Turkish troops, were quartered, to the number of 200 horse soldiers in Yondjalee, half an hour distant from Odandjor, 200 in Kop, and 100 in Shekagoob. The protection which they afforded was given to the Koords, and the reward they received was a share in the spoils.

The protection given by Turkish law is of a like nature, only

---

* Khozro, a well-to-do inhabitant of Prkhooss, near Lake Nazig (District of Akhlat), was a lucky exception. True, he did not exactly possess a gun, but he was suspected of having one. His house was searched, the floor dug up, the roof examined, in vain. Then he was imprisoned for a month and allowed to purchase his liberty by paying £70 in gold and signing a paper to the effect that he never had firearms of any kind.

incomparably more disastrous to those Armenians who venture to have recourse to it. Two or three instances, vouched for by a host of witnesses, verified by foreign consuls, and authenticated by official documents, will throw light enough for all practical purposes upon the strange forms assumed by Turkish justice in the provinces of Armenia.

Kevork Vartanian, of the village of Mankassar (Sandjak of Alashkerd), testified, among other things, as follows: "In 1892, a Koord, Andon by name, son of Kerevash (of the tribe of Tshalal), came with his comrades to my house and took five pounds in gold belonging to me, which I had saved up to buy seed corn with. I lodged a complaint against him, but the authorities dismissed me with contempt. Andon, hearing of my attempt to have him punished, came one night with twelve men, stood on our roof, and looking down through the aperture fired. My daughter-in-law, Yezeko, struck by a bullet, fell dead. Her two boys and my child Missak (two years old) likewise lost their lives then and there. Then the Koords entered the apartments and took my furniture, clothing, four oxen and four cows.* I hastened to the village of Karakilisse and complained to Rahim Pasha. Having heard my story, he said: 'The Hamadieh Koords are the Sultan's warriors. To do thus is their right. You Armenians are liars.' *And we were imprisoned.* We did not obtain our release until we had paid two pounds in gold.

"The following winter two hundred soldiers entered our village under the leadership of Rahim Pasha himself. He at once told us that it was illegal to complain of the doings of the Koords. Then he quartered himself and his troops upon us and demanded daily eight sheep, ten measures of barley, besides eggs, poultry, and butter. Forty days running our village supplied these articles of food gratis, receiving curses and blows for our pains. Rahim Pasha, angry with his host, Pare, for grumbling, had a copper vessel hung over the fire, and, when heated, ordered it to be placed on Pare's head. Then he had him stripped naked and little bits of flesh nipped out of his quivering arms with pincers.

"These ruffians had scarcely quitted our village when Aïpé Pasha with sixty horsemen took their places. Seeing that there were no more sheep to be had in the village, they slaughtered and ate our cows and oxen, and having inflicted much suffering upon us during six days, they too left. To whom could we address our complaints, seeing that the legally constituted authorities themselves perpetrated these things? Nothing was left for us but to quit the country, which we did?"

In the month of June, 1890, the village of Alidjikrek was the

---

* Cows, horses, &c., are frequently lodged in the apartment in which the inmates live and sleep. I have passed many a restless night in a spacious room along with horses, buffaloes, oxen, sheep and goats.

scene of a double crime. The Armenian shepherds who were tending the flocks of the villagers rushed in excitedly asking for help. "The Koords of Ibil Ogloo Ibrahim came up with their sheep and drove us out of the village pastures." It was one of the commonplaces of village life in Turkish Armenia. Four young men set out to reason with the Moslems and assert the rights of property; but scarcely had they reached the ground, when the Koords opened fire and killed one of the youths, named Hossep, on the spot. Another fell mortally wounded; his name, Haroothioon. Their comrades fled in horror to the village; the people, dismayed, abandoned their work; the parish priest and several of the principal inhabitants ran to the scene of the murder, others rode off to inform the gendarmes.

. The Zaptiehs (gendarmes), accompanied by an official, were soon on the spot. They found Hossep dead, and the parish priest, Der Ohannes, administering the last consolations of religion to the dying Haroothioon. They ordered the prayers to cease and menacingly asked, "Where are the Koordish murderers?" "They have fled," was the reply. "Indeed; probably you, dogs, have killed them, and buried them out of sight. You are all my prisoners." (Turning to the priest.) "You, too, come!" And they were all taken to Hassankaleh and thrown into the loathsome dungeon there. After a time they were transferred to the prison of Erzeroum.

The parish priest, Der Ohannes, was a well to do man. The process of systematic impoverishment was then only beginning. His brother, Garabed, and their ten comrades in misfortune, were likewise men of substance, and it seemed desirable to the officials that their property should change hands. They were left, therefore, to soak in the fetid vapours of a reeking Eastern prison-house. The time dragged slowly on, day by day, week by week, and month by month, till they seemed to have been completely forgotten. Their families were in an endless agony of fear, their affairs were utterly neglected, their health was wholly undermined. In this pandemonium they passed a year—the most horrible period of their lives.

Then they humbly besought their persecutors to help them to their liberty and to name the price. The terms were agreed to, and they were advised to send Koords to hunt up traces of the Koordish murderers whom they were accused of having murdered in turn. "If they be found you will be set free." The cost of this advice and of the ways and means of carrying it out amounted to about £400, which the prisoners were compelled to borrow at 40 per cent. interest.

The search was of course successful, Koordish and Turkish assassins, when their victims are Christians, having no need to hide their persons, no motive to hang their heads. What they do is well done These particular heroes were found enrolled in a battalion of his Majesty's favourite cavalry—the Hamidieh of Alashkerd. They confessed and did not deny; a cloud of witnesses—Turks and Koords of course, Christians being disqualified—testified in court in favour of the twelve Armenian prisoners, who were then set at liberty, with ruined fortunes and broken health. The sentence of the court set forth that the Armenians, charged with the crime of having killed certain Koords who had assassinated two Armenian villagers, had proved their innocence, the Koords in question having been discovered living and well, serving the Commander of the Faithful in the Hamidieh Corps.

. The Koordish murderers, about whose precious lives so much fuss was made, were left in peace, and they still continue to serve his Majesty the Sultan with the same zeal and contempt of consequences as before.

A dog will bark if another dog be shot in its presence. These Armenians did not even grumble; they simply called in the representatives of Imperial law and justice, who proceeded to deal with them as with murderers. But Christians in Armenia dare not aspire to be treated with the consideration shown to obedient dogs by goodnatured masters.

The stories told of these Koordish Hamidieh officers in general, and of one of them, named Mostigo, in particular, seemed so wildly improbable, that I was at great pains to verify them. Learning that this particular Fra Diavolo had been arrested and was carefully guarded as a dangerous criminal in the prison of Erzeroum, where he would probably be hanged, I determined to obtain, if possible, an interview with him, and learn the truth from his own lips. My first attempt ended in failure; Mostigo being a desperate murderer, who had once before escaped from jail, was subjected to special restrictions, and if I had carried out my original plan of visiting him in disguise, the probability is that I should not have returned alive. After about three weeks' tedious and roundabout negotiations, I succeeded in gaining the gaoler's ear, having first replenished his purse. I next won over the brigand himself, and the upshot of my endeavors was an arrangement tnat Mostigo was to be allowed to leave the prison secretly, and at night, to spend six hours in my room, and then to be re-conducted to his dungeon.

When the appointed day arrived the gaoler repudiated his part of the contract, on the ground that Mostigo, aware tnat his life was forfeited, would probably give the prison a wide berth if allowed to leave its precincts. After some further negotiations, however, I agreed to give two hostages for his return, one of them a brother Koord, whose life the brigand's notions of honour would not allow him to sacrifice for the chance of saving his own. At last he came to me one evening, walking over the roofs, lest the police permanently stationed at my door should espy him. I kept him all night, showed him to two of the most respectable Europeans in Erzeroum, and, lest any doubt should be thrown on my story, had myself photographed with him next morning.

The tale unfolded by that Koordish noble constitutes a most admirable commentary upon Turkish *régime* in Armenia. This is not the place to give it in full. One or two short extracts must suffice.

Q. " Now, Mostigo, I desire to hear from your own lips and to write down some of your wonderful deeds. I want to make them known to the 'hat-wearers.'" *

A. " Even so. Announce them to the Twelve Powers." †

There were evidently no misgivings about moral consequences; no fears of judicial punishment. And yet retribution was at hand; Mostigo was said to be doomed to death. Desirous of clearing up this point, I went on:

Q. "I am sorry to find that you are living in prison. Have you been long there?"

A. "I, too, am sorry. Five moths, but it seems an age."

Q. "These Armenians are to blame, I suppose?"

A. "Yes."

Q. " You wiped out too many of them, carried off their women, burned their villages, and made it generally hot for them, I am told."

A. (scornfully). "That has nothing to do with my imprisonment. I shall not be punished for plundering Armenians. We all do that. I seldom killed, except when they resisted. But the Armenians betrayed me and I was caught. That's what I mean. But if I be hanged it will be for attacking and robbing the Turkish post and violating the wife of a Turkish Colonel who is now here in Erzeroum. But not for Armenians! Who are they that I should suffer for them?"

After he had narrated several adventures of his, in the course of which he dishonored Christian woman, killed Armenian villagers, robbed the post and escaped from prison, he went on to say:

" We did great deeds after that : deeds that would astonish the Twelve Powers to hear told. We attacked villages, killed people who would have killed us, gutted houses, taking money, carpets, sheep and women, and robbed travellers. . . . Daring and great were our deeds, and the mouths of men were full of them."

Having heard the story of many of these " great deed," in some of which fifty persons met their death, I asked:

Q. "Do the Armenians ever offer you resistance when you take their cattle and their women?"

---

* The Koords calll all Europeans hat-wearers, and generally regard them with espect and awe.

† *I. e.*, to the whole universe.

A. "Not often. They cannot. They have no arms, and they know that even if they could kill a few of us it would do them no good, for other Koords would come and take vengeance; but when we kill them no one's eyes grow large with rage. The Turks hate them, and we do not. We only want money and spoil, and some Koords also want their lands, but the Turks want their lives. A few months ago I attacked the Armenian village of Kara Kipriu and drove off all the sheep in the place. I did not leave one behind. The villagers, in despair, did follow us that time and fire some shots at us, but it was nothing to speak of. We drove the sheep towards Erzeroum to sell them there. But on the way we had a fight near the Armenian village of Sheme. The peasants knew we had lifted the sheep from their own people, and they attacked us. We were only five Koords and they were many—the whole village was up against us. Two of my men—*rayahs** only—were killed. We killed fifteen Armenians. They succeeded in capturing forty of the sheep. The remainder we held and sold in Erzeroum."

Q. " Did you kill many Armenians generally ? "

A. " Yes. We did not wish to do so. We only want booty, not lives. Lives are of no use to us. But we had to drive bullets through people at times to keep them quiet ; that is, if they resisted."

Q. " Did you often use your daggers ?"

A. " No; generally our rifles. We must live. In autumn we manage to get as much corn as we need for the winter, and money besides. We have cattle, but we take no care of it. *We give it to the Armenians to look after and feed*."

Q. "But if they refuse ? "

A. " Well, we burn their hay, their corn, their houses, and we drive off their sheep, so they do not refuse. We take back our cattle in spring, and the Armenians must return the same number that they received."

Q " But if the cattle disease should carry them off ? "

A. " That is the *Armenians*' affair. They must return us what we gave them, or an equal number. And they know it. We cannot bear the loss. Why should not they ? Nearly all our sheep come from them."

After having listened to scores of stories of his expeditions, murders, rapes, &c., &c., I again asked: " Can you tell me some more of your daring deeds, Mostigo, for the ears of the Twelve Powers ? " to which I received this characteristic reply:

---

* The Koords are divided into *Torens* or nobles, who lead in war time, and possess and enjoy in peace; and *Rayahs*, who sacrifice their lives for their lords in all raids and feuds, and are wholly dependent on them at all times. A *rayah's* life may be taken by a *toren* with almost the same impunity as a Christian's.

"Once the wolf was asked: Tell us something about the sheep you devoured? and he said: I ate thousands of sheep, which of them are you talking about? Even so it is with my deeds. If I spoke and you wrote for two days, much would still remain untold."

This brigand is a Koord, and the name of the Koords is legion. *Ex uno disce omnes.* And yet the Koords have shown themselves to be the most humane of all the persecutors of the Armenians. Needing money, this man robbed; desirous of pleasure he dishonored women and girls; defending his booty, he killed men and women, and during it all he felt absolutely certain of impunity, so long as his victims were Armenians. Is there no law then? one is tempted to ask. There is, and a very good law for that corner of the globe were it only administered; for the moment he robbed the Imperial post and dishonored a Turkish woman, he was found worthy of death.

Laws, reforms and constitutions therefore, were they drawn up by the wisest and most experienced legislators and statesmen of the world, will not be worth the paper they are written on so long as the Turks are allowed to administer them without control. The proof is contained in the life and acts of Turkish officials any time during the past fifty years.

Here, for example, is an honorable record of an energetic administrator, his Excellency Hussein Pasha, Brigadier-General of his Majesty the Sultan, which will bear the closest scrutiny. Commanding a gang of Koordish brigands, which could be increased to about 2,000 men, he continually harassed the peaceful inhabitants of the province, plundering, torturing, violating, killing, till his name alone sent a thrill of terror to the hearts of all. The Armenians of Patnotz suffered so much from his depredations that they all quitted their village *en masse* and migrated to Karakilisse, where the Kaimakam resides; whereupon Hussein surrounded the house of the Bishop of Karakalisse with a large force and compelled him to send the people back. Even the Mohammedans felt so shocked at his doings, that tne Mussulman priest of Patnotz, Sheikh Nari, complained of him to the Vali (Governor-General) of Erzeroum. Hussein then sent his men, who murdered Sheikh Nari and frightened his daughter-in-law to death. In one expedition he carried off 2,600 sheep, many horses, kine, &c., took £500, burnt nine villages, killed ten men, and cut off the right hands, noses and ears of eleven others. Early in the year 1890 he raped five Christian girls of Patnotz, and in September and October of the same year he levied a contribution of £300 on the people of the same district. *For none of these crimes was he ever tried.* In December, 1890, he sent his brother to raise more money, which was done by raiding twenty-one villages of the Aintab District, the net result being £350 and 200 *batmans* of butter (≙ 3,000 lbs.). Hatsho, an

Armenian of Patnotz, who could not, or would not, contribute a certain sum to his coffer, had his house raided in his absence, and his wife and two children killed. All this time the gallant Hussein occupied the post and "discharged the duties" of a Mudir or Deputy Sub-Governor. One day he drove off 1,000 sheep and 7 yoke of buffaloes from Patnotz and Kizilkoh and sold them in Erzeroum to a merchant, after which he confiscated a fine horse belonging to Manook, an Armenian of Kizilkoh, and sent it as a present to the son of an Erzeroum judge. One night towards the end of February, 1891, Hussein, his nephew Rassoul, and others, entered the house of an Armenian, Kaspar, for the purpose of carrying off Kaspar's handsome daughter-in-law. The inmates, however, shouted for help, whereupon Hussein, raising his revolver, shot the young woman dead. A petition was presented asking that he be punished, but the Vali of Erzeroum declined to receive it, and Hussein was summoned to Constantinople, welcomed with cordiality, decorated by his Majesty, raised to the rank of Pasha, and appointed Brigadier-General. When the troops went to Moush and Sassoun last year, Hussein was one of the heroes, and when "order" was restored there, he returned to Patnotz with several young Sassounian girls whom he abducted, and he now lives happy and respected. No doubt there are missions which might be entrusted to a gentleman like Brigadier-General Hussein Pasha and men of his type. But is the government of a Christian people one of them? And if we assume that the then Vali of Erzeroum and the other administrators of the country were men of a much higher moral standard than he, of what avail were their noble character and admirable intentions, seeing that they allowed him to plunder, ravish, burn and kill unchecked? And is it reasonable to blame Hussein Pasha for deeds, after the perpetration of which, he was honored and promoted by the guardian of all law and order, the Commander of the Faithful?

Not all of the officials have the same tastes or the same degree of courage as his Excellency Hussein Pasha. There are others—many others no doubt—who, whatever their private proclivities may be, feel moved by their official sense of the fitness of things to cast about for a pretext for acts for which there could be no conceivable justification. And the follies which they commit in pursuit of this shadow would seem incredible were they not notorious. The following case has been inquired into and verified by the foreign representatives in Turkey. In the spring of 1893 Hassib Pasha, the Governor of Moush, feeling the need of some proofs of the disaffection of the Armenians of Avzoot and the neighboring villages, despatched Police Captain Reshid Effendi thither to search for arms. Reshid set out, made careful inquiries and diligently searched in the houses, on the roofs, under the ground, but in vain. There were no firearms anywhere. He returned and reported that the villagers had strictly observed the law forbidding them to possess weapons of any kind. But Hassib Pasha waxed wroth. "How dare you assert what I know to be untrue?" he asked. "Go back this minute and find the arms. Don't dare return without them!" The Police Captain again rode off to Avzoot and searched every nook and corner with lamps, so to say, turning the houses inside out. But he found nothing. Then he summoned the village Elder and said: " I have been sent to discover the hidden arms here. Tell me where they are." "But there are none." "There must be some." " I assure you you are mistaken." "Well, now listen. I have to find arms here, whether there are any or none, and I cannot return without them. Unless you deliver me some, I shall quarter myself and my men upon your village." This meant certainly plunder and probably rape. The Elder was dismayed. "What are we to do?" he asked. "We have no arms." "Go and get some then, steal them, buy them, but get them." Two or three persons were accordingly sent to the nearest Koordish village, where they purchased three cart-loads of old daggers, flintlock guns and rusty swords, which were duly handed over to Reshid. With these he returned to the Governor of Moush exulting. Hassib Pasha, seeing the collection, rejoiced exceedingly and said: "You see now, I was right. I told you there were arms hidden away there. You did not seek for them properly at first. Be more diligent in future."

Verto Popakhian, an inhabitant of the village of Khalil Tshaush (Khnouss), narrated the following, the story of his troubles, which throws a curious sidelight on Turkish justice and Armenian peasant-life generally:

"A Koord named Djundee endeavored to carry off my niece, Nazo, but we took her to Erzeroum, and gave her in marriage to an Armenian. We often have to give our young girls in marriage when they are mere children, eleven to twelve years old, or else dress them up in boys' clothes, to preserve them undefiled. Nazo's husband was the son of the parish priest of Hertev. The Koords vowed vengeance upon me for saving the girl thus. Djundee beat my brother so seriously that he was ill in bed for nearly six months, and he and his men drove off my cattle, burned our grain, threshing-floor, and hay, and ruined us completely. When the girl came home on a visit, Djundee and his Koords attacked the house, and carried her off. We complained to all the authorities in the place and in Erzeroum too. By the time they agreed to examine the girl publicly, she had borne a child to the Koord, and shame prevented her return. She remained a Mohammedan. We then bought a gun for our protection, the law forbidding firearms not existing yet. In 1893 we sold the gun to a Koord named Hadji Daho, but in 1894 the police came and demanded it. We said we had sold it, and the Koord bore out our assertion. He even showed it to them. But they arrested my brother and myself, and compelled us to give our two buffaloes in exchange for two guns, which they took away as incriminating proof of our guilt; and then they sent us to Erzeroum prison. We were kept here, suffering great hardships, for a long time. When eight months had passed away, my brother died of ill-treatment. Then they promised me my liberty in consideration of large bribes, which reduced me to absolute beggary. I had no choice. I gave them all they asked, leaving myself and family of nineteen persons completely destitute. *And then they condemned me to five years' imprisonment."*

Justice in all its aspects is rigorously denied to the Armenian. The mere fact that he dares to invoke it as plaintiff or prosecutor against a Koord or a Turk is always sufficient to metamorphose him into a defendant or a criminal, generally into both, whereupon he is invariably thrown into prison. In such cases the prison is intended to be no more than the halfway-house between relative comfort and absolute misery, the inmates being destined to be stripped of all they possess and then turned adrift. But what the prison really is cannot be made snfficiently clear in words. If the old English Star Chamber, the Spanish Inquisition, a Chinese opium den, the ward of a yellow fever hospital, and a nook in the lowest depths of Dante's Hell be conceived as blended and merged into one, the resulting picture will somewhat resemble a bad Turkish prison. Filth, stench, disease, deformity, pain in forms and degrees inconceivable in Europe, constitute the physical characteristics: the psychological include the blank despair that is final, fiendish, fierce malignity, hellish delight in human suffering, stoic self-sacrifice in the cultivation of loathsome vices, stark madness raging in the moral nature only—the whole incarnated in grotesque beings whose resemblance to man is a living blasphemy against the Deity. In these noisome dungeons, cries of exquisite suffering and shouts of unnatural delight continually commingle; ribald songs are sung to the accompaniment of heartrending groans; meanwhile the breath is passing away from bodies which had long before been soulless, and are unwept save by the clammy walls whereon the vapour of unimagined agonies and foul disease condenses into big drops and runs down in driblets to the reeking ground. Truly it is a horrid nightmare quickened into life.

Last March I despatched a friend of mine to visit the political prisoners in the Bitlis penitentiary, and to ask them to give me a succinct account of their condition. Four of them replied in a joint letter, which is certainly the most gruesome piece of reading I have beheld ever since I first perused a description of the Black Hole. Only the least sensational passages can be stripped of the decent disguise of a foreign language and exposed to the light of day. It is dated "Bitlis Prison, Hell, March 28 (April 9th), 1895," and begins thus:

"In Bitlis Prison there are seven cells, each one capable of containing from ten to twelve persons. The number they actually contain is from twenty to thirty. *There are no sanitary arrangements whatever.* Offal, vermin, and the filth that should find a special place elsewhere are heaped together in the same cell. . . . . The water is undrinkable. Frequently the Armenian prisoners are forced to drink 'Khwlitsh' water—*i. c.*, water from the tank in which the Mohammedans perform their ablutions. . . . ."

Then follows a brief but suggestive account of the treatment endured by the writers' comrades, many of whom died from the effects. For example: "Malkhass Aghadjanian and Serop Malkhassian of Avzoot (Moush) were beaten till they lost consciousness. The former was branded in eight places, the latter in twelve places, with a hot iron." The further outrage which was committed upon Serop must be nameless. "Hagop Seropian, of the village of Avzoot, was stripped and beaten till he lost consciousness; then a girdle was thrown round his neck, and having been dragged into the Zaptieh's room, he was branded in sixteen parts of his body with red-hot ram-rods." Having described other sufferings to which he was subjected, such as the plucking out of his hair, standing motionless in one place without food or drink till nature could hold out no longer, the writer goes on to mention outrages for which the English tongue has no name, and civilized people no ears. Then he continues:

"Sirko Minassian, Garabed Malkhassian, and Isro Ardvadzadoorian of the same village, having been violently beaten, were forced to remain in a standing position for a long time, and then had the contents of certain vessels poured upon their heads. Korki Mardoyan, of the village of Semol, was violently beaten; his hair was plucked out by the roots, and he was forced to stand motionless for twenty-four hours. Then Moolazim Hadji Ali and the gaoler, Abdoolkadir, forced him to perform the so-called *Sheitantopy*,* which resulted in his death. He was forty-five years of age. Mekhitar Saforian and Khatsho Baloyan of Kakarloo (Boolanyk) were subjected to the same treatment. Mekhitar was but fifteen and Khatsho only thirteen years old. Sogho Sharoyan, of Alvarindj (Moush), was conveyed from Moush to Bitlis prison handcuffed. Here he was cruelly beaten, and forced to maintain a standing position without food. Whenever he fainted they revived him with douches of cold water and stripes. They also plucked out his hair, and burned his body with red-hot irons. Then . . . (They subjected him to treatment which cannot be described.) . . . Hambartzoon Boyadjian, after his arrest, was exposed to the scorching heat of the sun for three days. Then he was taken to Semal, where he and his companions were beaten and shut up in a church. They

---

*Literally "Devil's ring." The hands are tightly bound together, and the feet, tied together by the great toes, are forced up over the hands. The remainder of the *Sheitantopy* consists of a severe torture and a beastly crime.

were not only not allowed to leave the church to relieve the wants of nature, but were forced to defile the baptismal fonts and the church altar. . . . Where are you, Christian Europe and America?"

The four signatures at the foot of this letter include that of a highly respected and God-fearing ecclesiastic.†

I am personally acquainted with scores of people who have passed through these prison mills. The stories they narrate of their experience there are gruesome, and would be hard to believe were they not amply confirmed by the still more eerie tales told by their broken spirits, their wasted bodies, and the deep scars and monstrous deformities that will abide with them till the grave or the vultures devour them. There is something so forbiddingly fantastic and wildly grotesque in the tortures and outrages invented by their gaolers or their local governors that a simple, unvarnished account of them sounds like the ravings of a diseased devil. But this is a subject upon which it is impossible to be explicit.

The manner in which men qualify for the Turkish prison in Armenia can be easily deduced from what has already been said. The possession of money, cattle, corn, land, a wife or daughter, or enemies, is enough. We are shocked to read of the cruelty of brutal Koords, who ride to a village, attack the houses, drive off the sheep, seize all the portable property, dishonor the women, and return leisurely home, conscious of having done a good day's work. We call it a disgrace to civilization, and perhaps the qualification is correct. But bad as it sounds, it is a mercy compared with the *Turkish* methods, which rely upon the machinery of the law and the horrors of the prison. A man whom poverty, nay, hunger, prevents from paying imaginary arrears of taxes, who declines to give up his cow or his buffalo as backsheesh to the Zaptiehs, who beseeches them to spare the honor of his wife or his daughter, is thrown into one of these dungeons, which he never leaves until he has been branded with the indelible stigma of the place. But let us take one of the usual and by no means most revolting cases of arrest and imprisonment as an illustration.

A young man from the village of Avzood (Moush District) went to Russia in search of work, and found it. He also married, and lived there for several years. Towards the close of 1892 he came back to his native village, and the police, informed that "an Armenian who has lived in Russia is returned," despatched four of their number under the orders of Isaag Tshaush to Avzood. They arrived two hours after sundown, and while three of them guarded the house where the young man was staying, the leader entered. Shots were heard immediately after, and the young Armenian and Isaag lay dead.

---

†As three of the writers are still in prison, prudence forbids me to publish their names, which are in the possession of our Foreign Office.

The authorities in Bitlis then sent a Colonel of the Zaptiehs to Avzood to see "justice" done. And it was done very speedily. The Colonel summoned the men of the village—none of whom were mixed up in the matter—and put them in prison. Then the officials deflowered all the girls and dishonored all the young women in Avzood, after which they liberated the men, except about twenty, whom they conveyed to the gaol of Bitlis. A few of these died there, and ten others were soon afterwards dismissed. Finally they decided to charge a young teacher, Markar, of the village of Vartenis with the murder of Isaag Tshaush, and as there was no evidence against him, the other prisoners were ordered to testify. Armenians have the reputation of being liars, but they certainly draw the line at swearing away an innocent man's life; and they refused in this case to commit the double crime of perjury and murder. Strenuous efforts were made to determine them; they were stripped naked, burned in various parts of the body with red-hot irons, till they yelled with pain. Then they were prevented from sleeping for several nights, and tortured acutely again, till, writhing and quivering, they promised to swear anything, everything, if once relieved from their agony. A document declaring that Markar was in the village when Isaag Tshaush arrived there, and that he had shot Isaag in their presence, was drawn up in their names. To this they duly affixed their seals. Meanwhile Markar himself was being tortured in another part of the prison.

When the trial came on and the incriminating document was read, the signatories stripped themselves in court, exhibited the ugly marks left by the red-hot irons, and called God to witness that that evidence of theirs, wrung from them by maddening torture, was a lie. Markar, on the other hand, declared that he was not in Avzood village at all on the night in question. But these statements were unavailing; he was hanged last year, and the "witnesses" condemned to various terms in fortified towns. Some of the women dishonored by the Zaptiehs died from the effects of the treatment to which they were subjected.

The gaolers grow rich on the money they wring from the inmates of the cells. The prison-keeper of Bitlis Prison, Abdoolkader, a wretch who, God having presumably made him, may be called a man, earns enormous sums in this way. He lately spent £500 on his house, and two or three Turkish merchants are said to be doing business on his capital, although his salary is only about 50s. a month. These sums are received as bribes, not for any positive return made to the prisoners, but for mere relief from torture employed solely for this purpose. The following case may give some idea of the nature of the relief thus highly paid for. Some five months ago three men of the village of Krtabaz were arrested and imprisoned.* The fact

---
* Their names are Vehret, Mardiross Der Kasparian, and Goolbeg.

that they were released without trial ten weeks later is evidence enough of their innocence of crime. They were taken to the prison of Hassankaleh. The room in which they were confined was over-crowded. The term overcrowding does not connote the same thing in Armenia as in European prisons. *They had no room to lie down at all.* Some Koordish prisoners confined in the same dismal den, who enjoyed special privileges, had but two and a half feet space to sleep in. In one corner of the dungeon a hole in the wall represented the prison-equivalent of sanitation, and these three Armenians were told that they must stand up by this hole, and might lean against the wall to sleep. *This they did for fifteen consecutive nights.* The stench, the filth, the vermin exceed all conception. After the lapse of fifteen days, by dint of starving themselves, they were enabled to give part of their food to some of the Koords, one of whom allowed the Armenians to take his place in turn during the day. This was not much, for the Koords themselves had only sitting space, about 2½ feet long; still it did afford relief. But the Koord was severely punished for this benevolence or enterprise. His rations of bread were cut off, and he was put in irons for several days. The men he thus befriended, who now aver they owe their lives to him, were notables of their village, and innocent persons to boot, who were released some weeks later because "they had done no wrong."

It is no easy thing for an Armenian man to cross the frontier and enter Russia, if he possess a gold or silver coin or an article of clothing; nor for a woman to leave the country without first undergoing indignities, the mere mention of which should make a man's blood boil with shame and indignation. "Oh, but these things are not felt so acutely by Armenians as they would be by Europeans," said an English lady to me a few days ago: "the wind is tempered to the shorn lamb, don't you know." It may be so; but I have seen and conversed with hundreds and hundreds of Armenian women lately, and I found no signs of the tempering process. Whatever vices or virtues may be predicated of Armenian women, chastity must be numbered among their essential characteristics. They carry it to an incredible extreme. In many places an Armenian woman never even speaks to any man but her husband, unless the latter is present. Even to her nearest and dearest male relatives and connections she has nothing to say; and her purity, in the slums of Erzeroum as in the valleys of Sassoun, is above suspicion. Yet these are the people who are being continually outraged by brutal Koords and beastly Turks, oftentimes until death releases them. But the difficulty of emigrating from Turkey, with money, clothing, or women, will be best understood in the light of a few concrete examples. Not that the Turks object to their leaving. On the contrary—and this is the most conclusive proof of the existence of the Plan of Extermination—they actually drive them over the frontier and then persistently refuse to allow them to return.

Sahag Garoyan, questioned as to the reasons why he and his family of ten persons emigrated from his village of Kheter (Sandjak of Bayazid), deposed as follows:

"We could not remain because we were treated as beasts of burden by Rezekam Bey, son of Djaffer Agha, and his men, who belong to his Majesty's Hamidieh corps, and can therefore neither be punished nor complained of. I emigrated towards the end of last year. Rezekam had come with his followers, as if it were war time, and taken possession of the houses of the Armenians, driving the occupants away. Only seven families were allowed to stay on. The others, having no place to go to, took refuge in the church. We had to feed the Koords for three months, giving them our corn, sheep, &c., and keeping their cattle in fodder. We had to serve some of them as beasts of burden.* Rezekam himself paid a weekly visit to the village of Karakilisse, and levied a contribution of £10 Turkish on the inhabitants, besides hay, barley, &c., for his men. At last, unable to bear this burden any longer, we addressed a complaint to the authorities. They told us to be gone. Then a Koord, named Ghazas Teamer, ordered us to sign a document setting forth that we were prosperous and happy. This was to be sent to Constantinople, as he wished to be appointed Yoozbashi of the Hamidiehs. No one signed the paper, whereat Teamer grew angry, and killed Avaki and his brother. Five months later he killed Minass, son of Kre, of the village of Mankassar. When the winter came on last year, Rezekam Bey imprisoned our neighbor Sarkiss, son of Sahag, had his head plunged in cold water and dried; after that it was steeped in petroleum and his hair burned off. Then he endeavored to violate Sara, Sarkiss' sister, but she was smuggled away in time. Rezekam's servant, Kheto, dishonored Moorad's wife; and a few days later entered the house of Abraham, an inhabitant of the same village, commanding him to go and work for Rezekam Bey. Abraham's wife, who was about to become a mother, begged that he might be allowed to stay at home; but Kheto kicked her in the stomach, and she was delivered of a dead child an hour or so after. Oh, we could not live there—not if we were beasts, instead of Christians."

Mgirdeetch Mekhoyan, aged thirty-five, of the village of Koopegheran (Sandjok of Bayazid), deposed: "I emigrated in 1894 because Aipa Pasha came with forty Koordish families, demolished our church, and took everything we had" The same story, with variations, comes from every Sandjak, almost from every village of the

---

*This is no uncommon thing in Armenia.

five Armenian provinces. Bedross Kozdyan, aged fifty-five, of the village of Arog (Sandjak of Van), testified:

"I left my village and my country with my family in August, last year (1894), because we were driven away by the Koords under Kri, son of Tshalo, who was abetted by the Turkish authorities. He first came and violated three girls and three young married women, whom he took away in spite of their cries and prayers Three Armenians tried to protect the wretched women, who implored them not to let them go. But the Koords killed the three on the spot. Their names were Sarkiss, Khatsho, and Keveark. Next day he and his men drove off the sheep of the villagers. We complained to the Governor of Van, but he said he could not move in the matter. Ten days later the Koords came again, and carried away our wheat, barley, and live stock, and burned the hay which they could not transport. Then they knocked down the altar of our church, hoping to find gold and silver hidden away there. We again besought the authorities to protect us, but they replied, 'We'll slaughter you like sheep if you dare to come again with your complaints against good Mohammedans.' Then we took what we could with us and set out for Russia. When we reached Sinak six armed Koords attacked us, robbed us of everything we had, and sent us over the frontier with nothing but our clothes."

The Plan of Extermination is obviously working smoothly and well. The Christian population is decimated, villages are changing hands almost as quickly as the scenes shift in a comic opera, and the exodus to Russia and the processions to the churchyard are increasing. This is not the place to give a list of *islamised* villages, but a typical case may help to convey an idea of the process that is going on even now. In the province of Alashkerd, which borders upon Russia, there are five villages to the east of Karakilisse, named respectively, Khedr (or Kheter), Mangassar, Djoodjan, Ziro and Koopkheran. These villages Eyoob Pasha sent his sons to occupy. Koords of the Zilanlee tribe, they are all officers in the Hamidieh corps. General Eyoob has three sons, Rezgo Bey, Khalid Bey and Yoossoof Bey, and these gallant officers with their followers set out last spring and took the villages for themselves. There were about 400 Armensan houses there at the time, or, say roughly, some 3,000 Christian inhabitants. Thre is not one there to-day. Only one individual, named Avedis Agha, has remained, and even he lives not in one of the four villages, but in Yoondjaloo. He was a wealthy man when the Koords arrived; he is indigent now. The Armenians were completely driven out in the course of a few months by methods which may be termed somewhat drastic. For example : one day the Koords met Markar, son of Ghoogo, in the fields carrying home his corn. They demanded his *araba* (cart). He replied that it was engaged now, as they could see for themselves, but that he would give it later on. They killed him on the spot for disobedience, and threw his body on the cart. Thirty villagers went with their children to complain to the Kaimakam in Karakilisse. The Kaimakam caused them to remain waiting in the open air for eleven days before he would hear them. And having heard them, he told them to go—to Kussia.

In the Vilayet of Bitlis (Kaza of Boolanyk and Sandjak of Moush) there is a village named Kadjloo, which, being interpreted, means "Village of the Cross." It is a village of the Crescent now. The means by which the sudden change was effected are identical in character with those already described. Mohammed Emin led a number of Koords (outcasts from the Djibranlee and Hassnanlee tribes) against the village, took it, so to say, by storm, and, to use their own picturesque expression, "sat down in it." Happily it is situated only five miles distant from the seat of the Turkish Deputy-Governor, but, unhappily for the people, he refused to move a finger, and they were all driven off like sheep. Perhaps this is one of the cases in which the wind is tempered to the shorn sheep?

Then the conquerors set about raiding the neighboring villages, and in particular Piran, which is about a mile further off. These would likewise have changed hands had it not been for a bright idea of one of the chief villagers, at whose suggestion a Koord named Assad Agha was invited to come and quarter his men in Piran, *accepting for himself twenty corn-fields, ten meadows*, and a spacious two-story house, which was built expressly for him by an architect from Bitlis, in return for which he undertook to protect the Armenians from Mohammed Emin and his merry men.

Three hundred and six of the principal inhabitants of the District of Khnouss gave me a signed petition when I was leaving Armenia, and requested me to lay it before "the humane and noble people of England." In this document they truly say:

"We now solemnly assure you that the butchery of Sassoun is but a drop in the ocean of Armenian blood shed gradually and silently all over the Empire since the late Turko-Russian war. Year by year, month by month, day by day, innocent men, women and children have been shot down, stabbed, or clubbed to death in their houses and their fields, tortured in strange, fiendish ways in fetid prison cells, or left to rot in exile under the scorching sun of Arabia. During the progress of that long and horrible tragedy no voice was raised for mercy, no hand extended to help us. That process is still going on, but it has already entered upon its final phases, and the Armenian people are at the last gasp. Is European sympathy destined to take the form of a cross upon our graves?"

I have also received two touching appeals from the women of Armenia, sealed with their seals, and addressed to their sisters of

England. What *they* ask is indeed little—that they be protected from dishonor. And, until the General Elections gave us a strong Government, which knows its own mind, it seemed as if these women were asking for the moon.

On November 7th last a Turk of the city of Bayazid asked Avedis Krmoyan to pay a little debt. The Armenian, not having the money at the time, besought his creditor to wait a few weeks. The Turk refused, and insisted on taking Krmoyan's wife as a pledge that the money would be paid. Entreaties and tears were unavailing; the woman was carried off, and then forced to become a Moslem. She can never return to her husband again.

In the village of Khosso Veran (Bassen) a girl named Selvy was seized by a Turk as security for a debt contracted by her father. The creditor kept her three months and dishonored her; nor would he consent to set her free until Giragoss Ohannissean went bail for her. As the debt, however, is unpaid, the Turk has a mortgage on her still. This sort of thing cannot be said to be uncommon, for although I knew but three cases of it from personal knowledge, I heard of more than a score in different parts of Armenia.

It is not only absolutely useless, but often positively dangerous, to complain to the officials, who, from high to low, take an active part in this Oriental "sport" themselves. The Kiateeb of Alai entered the house of Ohannes Goolykian (village of Karatshoban in Khnouss) in the broad daylight, and raped the daughter of Ohannes, who was fifteen years old, and then sent her off to Trebizond. Her father complained, besought the authorities to restore her, and it is only fair to say that, so far as I know, he was not punished for his temerity.

The Deputy-Governor of Arabghir actually arrested and expelled a number of the men of the town whose wives were considered to be among the most handsome women in Armenia. He next approached the latter, but was received with the scorn he deserved. Then these women shut themselves up in their houses, refusing to allow him or his men to enter, whereupon he told them, publicly and shamelessly, that if they wished their husbands to return, they must yield to his desires.

The following case is one in which I took a very lively interest, because I am well acquainted with the victim and her family. Her name is Lucine Mussegh, her native village Khnoossaberd. Born in 1878, Lucine was sent at an early age to the Amercian Missionary School at Erzeroum, where she was taught the doctrines of evangelical Christianity, her father, Aghadjan Kemalian, having always manifested a strong sympathy for Protestantism. Armenian girls are in chronic danger of being raped by Turks and Koords, and Armenian parents are continually scheming for the purpose of shielding them from this calamity which, as we have seen, occasionally results in death. The means usually employed are very early marriages or attempts to pass off the girls as boys.* I have known children to be taken from school, married, allowed to live a few months with their husbands or wives, and then sent back to school again. This is what happened to Lucine, who, taken from school at the age of fourteen, was wedded to a boy of her own age, Milikean by name, and having lived some time with him under his father's roof, was sent to the Protestant school once more. One night, during her husband's absence from home, she was seized by some men, dragged by the hair, gagged, and taken to the house of Hussni Bey. *This man is the son of the Deputy-Governor of the place.* He dishonored the young woman, and sent her home next day, but her husband refused to receive her any more, and she is now friendless and alone in the world.†

The massacre of Sassoun sends a shudder to the hearts of the most callous. But that butchery was a divine mercy compared with the hellish deeds that are being done every week and every day of the year. The piteous moans of famishing children; the groans of old men who have lived to see what can never be embodied in words; the piercing cries of violated maidenhood, nay, of tender childhood; the shrieks of mothers made childless by crimes compared with which murder would be a blessing; the screams, scarcely human, of women writhing under the lash; and all the vain voices of blood and agony that die away in that dreary desert without having found a responsive echo on earth or in heaven, combine to throw Sassoun and all its horrors into the shade.

Such are the things for which we are morally responsible; and in spite of the circumstances that the late Liberal Governmeut was in possession of these and analagous facts, Lord Kimberley found it impossible to have them remedied and unadvisable to have them published. There is fortunately good reason to believe that Lord Salisbury, who alone among English statesmen seems accurately to gauge all the difficulties of this thorny question, will find efficacious means of putting a sudden and a speedy end to the Armenian Pandemonium.

---

*In the village of Ishkhoe, for instance, the daughter of Tepan Agha was brought up as a boy. She was arrested and imprisoned some time ago in Erzeroum, for this, too, is a crime.

†She gave me an appeal to the women of England signed by herself, together with her photograph.

www.ingramcontent.com/pod-product-compliance
Lightning Source LLC
Chambersburg PA
CBHW030709110426
42739CB00031B/1443